The Battle
of the
Mind
The Kyle Robinson Story

Vivian Robinson

Kingdom Builders Publications LLC

ISBN: 979-8-218-47264-1 Soft Copy

LCCN: 2024915938

Printed in the USA

Authored by
Vivian Robinson

Adaptation
Louise Smith

Editor
Wanda Brown
Kingdom Builders Publications

Cover Design
LoMar Designs

Photographers
Heirloom photographs

Contact
vivian277246@yahoo.com

The Battle of the Mind: The Kyle Robinson Story

CONTENTS

CHAPTER 1

Kyle's Birth

It was the first month of 2011 when I felt GOD speaking to me to author a book about a tragic and devastating occurrence in our family. I was on my knees early one Sunday morning about 5 a.m. I was about to begin a 21 day fast to get instructions for my outreach ministry. I was given explicit instructions to draft a book, and to teach a four-week session on spiritual warfare for the radio ministry. One month after the tragedy, God's download to my spirit was even more clear. I was to do a four-week teaching on the tragedy and the spiritual warfare that went with it.

This devastating life change occurred December 15, 2009. This was the darkest day of my life! Everyone who knew us was devastated about this tragedy.

I am Vivian and my husband is Bertram. We are sharing the traumatic death of our second child, Kyle.

First off, without sounding mysterious and scary, I am a seer. There are unique gifts to people given by the CREATOR, not necessarily for themselves, but for the benefit of other people. God gave me a special power, and it is the gift of prophecy. God shows me events or scenes into people's lives, and they could be warned of things or a particular event to come. Prophecy is not just to forth-tell what God has already spoken in the Scriptures, but prophecy is also given to foresee the present or future of a matter or of a person.

Even though I am a minister, an evangelist, and have this powerful prophetic anointing, it couldn't help me on this particular day, and nothing prepared me for the tsunami that flooded and swept through our lives. I never saw it coming. As strong as my personal relationship is with God, He didn't give me a sign; He didn't speak to me; I mean HE said ABSOLUTELY NOTHING!

I know that all who are born, will also die, but if I knew in advance my son would die in his prime and in the way he did, I would have made the request to God not to take him, but to take me instead; only because I have lived longer, I know more, and I wouldn't want death for any of my children before me.

I was confident in my prayer life; I was confident in His answer to my prayers; yes I thought I had it like that. The relationship between the Lord and me were close and awesome. We conversed all the time. I've been through many trials and tribulations in my lifetime, and I know they come to make us strong, but this is one, I never wanted to go through. What person (parent} would? It is felt in minds across the globe that children bury their parents, not the other way around. For those of you who have lost a child, you know there is no feeling like it. I just felt removed from life, and living. I was merely breathing and existing. I was an empty shell; completely numb.

I asked the Father God, "Why didn't you let me know?"

He said, "If I had told you, there was nothing that could've been done about it, because it was in my perfect plan." I had to give in to the idea that I don't know everything, that I can't know everything; Only God is omniscient. He had that part sown up. Therefore, I had to submit my authority to Him and trust the process. So, I said,

"Yes, Lord, I know you are too wise to make a mistake."

Let me introduce you to the love of my life, Bertram. He and I met at eleven years old. Bertram's aunt was our pastor. She often brought her nephews and nieces to church and Bertram was one of the nephews. As a result, we saw each other every week, and we grew up together. We developed a friendship and became childhood sweethearts. He was my first and only boyfriend in life. We later married.

Our first child of five was a beautiful baby girl, born 1985. We were immensely proud and happy parents. Then we were blessed with 4 more amazing children of which all whose names started with "K". I don't know what it was about the letter K, but that was that.

Kashara
Kyle
Kevin
Kayla
Keenan

We pride ourselves as great partners and great parents. Fifteen months later, came Kashara's baby brother, Kyle.

When I was in labor with Kyle, his heart rate dropped, and it really scared me. I had all vaginal births with my five children. I took no medicine because I worked in the medical field and knew of too many complications and side effects from the drugs offered to pregnant women. I didn't want anything to happen to my children. I heard the nurse saying that his fetal heart rate was dropping. She went to get Dr. Chanda.

My husband was there for all our children's births except Kyle's. This was only because he did not get the message in time that I was in labor, so he came afterwards. It was just me and Jesus. I prayed, "Lord, let him be all right."

When Kyle came out of the birth canal, the umbilical cord was wrapped around his neck seven times. My heart dropped when I saw it, but thank God he was okay. It's good to have Jesus in your life. Kyle was highly active when I was carrying him in the womb. So he was a fighter, even then.

 After our son's transition, Jesus carried me and ministered to me. He reminded me of how Satan tried to steal my baby at birth, but Jesus said NO! Thank You Jesus!

It's a good thing to learn this. Every adult was once a child. As with our parents, we were their children, yet we didn't actually belong to our parents, we were the property of the Lord. So it is when our children are born, they don't belong to us, they belong to God. We are all the Lord's. At our children's dedication, we gave them back to God for His use and or His glory.

For whether we live, we live unto the Lord; and whether we die, we die unto the Lord: whether we live therefore, or die, we are the Lord's. **Romans 14:8**

Kyle was born on a Tuesday evening around 6:30 pm on a hot August day, on the 12th of the month. I was in labor for about 12 hours. He came in weighing 6 lbs. 1 ounce, and twenty-one inches long. He was born with a head full of hair. For the most part, he was happy. All babies have their share of irritabilities at times, and Kyle was no deferent in that regard.

My husband was super proud of having his first son. I asked if he wanted him to be named after him?

He said, "No. Let him have his own name," so there it was. We named him the longest name out of all of our five children. I selected his first name from the lead male character of the movie The Terminator. It was Kyle Reese, the soldier that Sarah Connor fell in love with. If you are a fan of The Terminator, you would know that. I love the movie and all the sequels that followed. I came up with Kyle Christopher and his father added Edwin. So his full name was Kyle Christopher Edwin Robinson. I know we got carried away, but he was the first boy.

The two siblings were incredibly beautiful and loving babies. They got along well together. Kashara loved being a big sister to her little brother. They built a bond which became inseparable.

Kyle learned early the comforts of his fingers. This baby came out the womb sucking on his 2nd finger; however, I switched that finger to his thumb due to his 2nd finger was raw from sucking on it.

Kyle continued sucking his thumb until he was 11 years old. That was a secret nugget never to be shared in front of his friends, of course. As he got older he sucked his thumb to comfort himself mostly at night.

He was a happy baby and after a month, he slept

all night. He started teething at 10 months, and started talking and walking at 11 months.

His Pre-Kindergarten days were at the YMCA. He loved playing with other children, toy trucks, cars, trains, guns, running around, laughing, and just having fun.

At 6 or 7 years old, the elementary school where he attended, considered that because he was fidgety, he had ADHD, but I did not receive that, so instead of the brutal medications the doctors would prescribe for this diagnosis, he was given lots of hugs, kisses, prayers, and encouragement.

He used to struggle with his homework and get frustrated and cry. He didn't think that he was as smart as the other children. I used to work with all my children with their school work. One day I told him to dry his tears, encouraging him to know he was just as smart as any other child. It's just sometimes some people have to work a little harder to achieve their goals. I said, "When people tell you that you can't do something, you prove them wrong, and then you accomplish it." From that day, he dried his tears and became an achiever. So, everything Kyle did, he put his best effort in it and did an excellent job. He had God in his life as well. *I can do all things through Christ that strengthens me* (**Philippians 4:13 KJV**). If God be for us, he's more than the entire world against us.

Kyle was ambitious, and he worked hard. At age 12, he had a paper route. We lived in Connecticut, so it snowed a lot, but he made effective use of his time and the weather by shoveling snow. He also raked other people's lawns for extra money, and helped his Aunt Geana clean toys at her daycare. He was a lot like his father, he liked to stay busy.

During Bertram and my friendship, I saw how Bertram moved about, and how he did various kinds of jobs. When Bertram was eleven, he worked on a newspaper route, shoveled snow, raked people's yards and other odd jobs.

Watching our boy as he grew, I'd have to say, he mirrored his dad in so many areas when he was young. Just like his dad, Kyle was never without money. They were romantics, industrious, family men, and temperamental. The similarities between these gentlemen were uncanny.

My husband instilled a lot of good morals by his own lifestyle and the teachings of the Scriptures. I can remember Bertram spending quality and quantity time with Kyle, as the first son, teaching and showing him how to do certain things methodically, like how to be responsible. He taught all of his sons about responsibility, about their bodies and sex. These things only men can instruct boys. I commend my husband; he did a fantastic job. I could not teach the fellas those type of things because I am a woman, but from the woman's prospective, I could teach the value and the respect to a man, how to treat a lady. Those were the same things I was teaching the girls, Like how to be godly young women. how to be domestic like cooking and cleaning the house, washing clothes, having good personal hygiene, living a life of celibacy, how to show respect, and be respected, how not to settle for just anything, and how to save themselves for marriage.

Kyle also had a close relationship with his father. They talked quite a bit and spent a host of time together. Kyle, I believe enjoyed modeling his dad. I saw the resemblance between he and his father. My husband loves all of his children dearly. Kyle was a generous giver to both his parents for their special holidays like Father's Day, Mother's Day and our birthday.

Kyle definitely was a momma's boy. He loved his

mother; God help you if you tried to hurt his mother. I used to call him the protector. He not only defended me, but his whole family. We were a sensitive subject to him, so people had to be careful of what they say about family. He was every parent's dream son. Kyle and I often talked on the phone. We had a close relationship as do with all of my children.

Kyle was a right-brainer; a creative guy. He was artistic, and it showed in the pictures he drew. Not just from a parent's view, was he good, but he was genuinely special. He had such beautiful artwork.

He was an exceptionally talented musician. By 12 years old, he could play the keyboard and drums. At 17 years old, he played the trombone, baritone, and saxophone. He also could sing and

He would come out to play the drums for the outreach ministry I was assigned to. He was very supportive of the ministry, and anything he was asked to do, he did. Kyle never denied his mother or the ministry, however I did not realize how much Satan was attacking my son's mind and the spiritual warfare he was going through. I now believe that my son suffered in silence.

Although he was a little precocious, ambitious, and talented, Kyle was my quiet and serious child. His siblings were a little more on the silly side, and of course, they could make him laugh. We're a remarkably close family. Kyle would often talk to his siblings and was very protective of the family.

CHAPTER 2

Family Introductions

Let me introduce you to the rest of the family and a few friends. While Kyle and his dad resembled each other in looks and actions, I'd have to say Kyle's features were most like mine.

A rich nugget to keep: Parents, please remember that children are God's beautiful blessings, so cherish them while you have them. I thank God that I have a close relationship with all my children, but Kyle and I were exceptionally close. There was just something so largely different about him. He seemed to give and get lots more hugs and kisses.

A few predominant things we instructed our children was never to lie, always tell the truth, no matter what. We were strict about moral values. We also taught to respect the elders, the GOLDEN RULE: do unto others as you would have them do unto you, to always be kind to others, and never take anything that does not belong to you. We also taught the children that siblings do not call each other out of their names, that family always stick together, no matter what happens! We taught them also to love everybody and do not be biased against anybody because of the color of their skin. Prejudice is not acceptable to God under any circumstances.

Another lesson we taught the children when they were young was how to pay their tithes. When Kyle did his little odd jobs at 11 years old, I had him pay a tenth of his earning to the church. So, if he had $10, I had him pay $1.00 for tithes. I took him to the scripture, Malachi 3:8-12 and explained it to him. I told him that he would always be blessed and want for nothing if he obeyed God's Word. He was always blessed throughout his youth and had God's favor on his life.

At age 16, Kyle got a part-time job. In order to teach him responsibility, we opened up a savings account for him and taught him to put some of his money in the bank. He paid his tithes, contributed $20 to the house, and spent some on himself. We never let him waste all his money. We taught him that nothing in life is free. God told us to be wise stewards. He was also taught to fast at least twice a week for a half day until lunch. Our Pastor told him the importance of praying and reading his Bible. So we tried to instill as much of God's Word into him as a youth as possible.

Kyle was an honest, respectful and noble young man. He knew how to respect women. Like his dad, he was romantic.

All the children got saved and filled with the Holy Ghost when they were young. Kashara at 12, Kyle at 11, Kevin at 10, Kayla at 9, and Keenan at 7 years old.

Pastor Stovall was doing an Old Testament burnt offering ceremony and told the congregants to write what they wanted from the Lord. Then he instructed them to fold the paper and throw it in this metal bucket. I wrote that I wanted God to save all of our children and fill them with the Holy Ghost. The participating congregants threw their requests in the bucket. Pastor said that if the smoke goes up, God has accepted the burnt offering. If it goes to the side, He did not. So he prayed over it and threw a match in the bucket; the papers were burning, and the smoke went up. You see, God did exactly what He said He would do. He saved all of our children. Kyle got saved at 11 years old and received the Holy Ghost.

He was a very obedient child and never gave his father and me any problems growing up.

That being said, girls loved him because he was incredibly handsome. He was kind of shy and just smiled a lot when girls flirted with him.

Kyle was remarkably connected to his brothers. He would come and pick up Keenan and take him to Six Flags, Chucky Cheese. He spent time with Kevin and also took him for rides. He told him to stay away from drugs and drinking because it would lead to terrible things. He also encouraged him to listen to his mom. Kyle also told Keenan to stay away from drugs, alcohol and warned him not to be so anxious to leave home. He wanted his brothers to learn from the choices he'd made, all not good.   He told Kayla to stay away from boys and if any of them messed with her to tell him. He just talked to Kashara in general because she was the oldest. He also, told her things he felt he couldn't tell anybody else.

In 2008, Kyle taught himself how to cut hair. He practiced on himself, then he cut both Kevin and Keenan's hair.

Kyle played sports and had lots of friends. In high school, he played football, basketball, track and field. Kyle was very Athletic and excelled at every sport, especially track. Track he ran the 100 meter, 200 meter, 400 meter relay and won several medals and went to the state championship several times. He was fast; he was the anchor on the 400 meter relay team.

He was a little quiet, but generally happy and very friendly. I don't think I would categorize Kyle as a temper tantrum kind of guy, but let's just say he was passionate about certain things. I saw his capacity to be a little irritable when he was a baby and toddler, and as he grew up to be a nice young man, that capacity was still present a little.

Kyle had friends, but his best friends were Joey and Kory. They met at the beginning of high school and always hung out together. Kyle and Joey enjoyed sleepovers at each other's houses and attended each other's family gatherings. Jeremy and Cody were his other great friends. Joey was probably the best friend because they were like brothers.

CHAPTER 3

Jobs and First Encounter

Three things our son enjoyed when he was young was Christmas, a good birthday party, and movie night. I believe for him; he loved the noise of fellowship with family and friends plus we can't leave out the attention he would get at our gatherings. I mean what child doesn't like Christmas. The story of Christmas, the colors and lights, snow and all that comes along with gift giving and gift receiving. For the holidays, there were usually some good friends, family, and good food. He loved food, but he really loved CAKE! I made his favorite cake every year for his birthday, which was a vanilla cake with chocolate frosting. That boy had an insatiable appetite for sweets. Let's just say he had a very addictive sweet tooth. The other was Sunday Night Movie Night. We started this tradition when the kids were young. We all got together and watched a movie, had popcorn, juice or Kool-Aid, talk and laughed a lot. Then Kyle introduced us to the character Madea, of Madea's Class Reunion, a stage play by Tyler Perry.

Sometime later, Kyle brought Madea's Family Reunion over for family night. We've gotten hooked on Tyler Perry's plays and movies. We have so many fond memories of laughter with our family. He grew up with close family ties. He was taught that family sticks together, no matter what.

Kyle was a one woman man. He had a couple of girlfriends in his junior and senior high school years. He dated a Tasha and took her to the Jr. Prom. He was gallant and debonair. He bought the usual prom gift to impress his date; a beautiful corsage flower. He was nervous about meeting her father because he was a pastor, but they looked gorgeous together. Tasha was very pretty.

As a teen, Kyle had already done yard jobs, of which he loved, and knew he was good at it. He wasn't new to landscaping because he started landscape work as a pre-teen, and it carried all the way out to the summer before his senior year of high school and he continued working with his good friend Joey. He grew up with Joey. When Kyle graduated, he continued doing landscaping until the autumn season when he lost his job for the first time. The reason he was let go was because one of the workers made a statement against him and the boss sided with the other worker instead; maybe it was because of seniority, or a more disturbing issue; prejudice, who can tell. He was an incredibly good worker, so this irritated him. I encouraged him to be patient and God would bless him with another landscaping job. I told him he could even have his own landscaping business one day. There were a few obstacles with bosses for whatever reasons, here and there, so he eventually ended up with his own landscaping business.

He did a beautiful job landscaping. He did yard grooming for our home and for the church along with some people I worked with at the Hospital. They all gave high kudos that he'd done a beautiful job, so getting the job with True Green was a blessing. It allowed him to work in a profession he liked.

Talk about persistence, there was a time when Kyle found a job in Massachusetts and he would ride his bike to work from Connecticut every day, (13 miles each way). His father and I worked at various times, and were unable to get him to work. He did not let transportation stop him. He faithfully went to work every day until he got enough money to buy a car. That was the type of young man he was.

Kyle Christopher Edwin Robinson graduated from High School, June 2, 2004. He had served in a few jobs as a young man. His odd jobs, True Green, Yankie Candle, and his own landscaping company. College is not for everyone, and for our son, college was not his career choice.

He moved away from home after High School graduation. He decided to move in with some of his friends. It was against our thought process on his behalf, but he was getting older and wanted his freedom. We can't keep our children under our wings forever.   After moving out, he began hanging out with his friends and started to change. We trained him up in the Word, but you have to let your children grow up and make their own decisions and mistakes. We prayed they would remember what was taught to them about salvation. His father and I did our job and now all we could do was to trust God to do His part. There is a God side and a man side. We can't do God's side, and God will not do our side, but HE is there to assist us as we do the human side.

We felt that Kyle, while a church boy, was about to embark onto a new world, filled with wolves and unbelievers; he'd move from a town to a city of uncharted waters; being stunted in a real and unprotected world.

I presumed that he would not handle new growing pains, like being away from his family and the familiarities of his surroundings well. He moved to Massachusetts with all the values we instilled in him. I tried to warn him that unbelievers or sinners won't treat him like God's people.

"They will lie and use you, mistreat you, and think nothing of it because this is what unbelievers do. They do not have Jesus in their lives, and we know that Satan is the God of this world and is their father. We know that when our children leave church they are prey for Satan. The devil is waiting with his snares, hooks, and his imps to try and destroy those who belong to God." In the scripture, **1st Peter 5:8**, it says, "*Your adversary the devil, as a roaring lion, walketh about seeking whom he may devour.*"

I asked Kyle to stay connected with us. I would feel better if I could just know he was all right. As mothers, we keep our children in our thoughts, prayers, and on our minds. It's hard to let them go sometimes; well especially in the beginning. We want to always be their protectors. As parents, we become sometimes zealous and overprotective, leaving God out of the equation, feeling as it is our sole purpose to shield our children and adult children.

Our son, for the sake of his parent's request, did call occasionally. However, I detected a change in his behavior. He was later introduced to alcohol and marijuana by these new friends. He stopped going to church. His dad said to him as a youngster to be careful who he called his friends because some people are really your enemies. In other words, they don't mean you any good. They're just in your life to get what they can out of you, use you, or discredit you. Remember that they are unbelievers and Satan will use them against you. Anyway, he told Kyle to call these people associates. How can two walk together except they agree? So don't call everybody your friend. Even some so-called Christians don't mean you any good.

Then we noticed little by little, Kyle became quieter, more serious, and laughed even less. I prayed for his safety because he was not living in a safe neighborhood. There had been some gang shootings going on in Massachusetts and a lot of young people were dying. Even one of the members in our church had tragically lost their twin sons within a month of each other from gang shootings. It was a very scary time for us. I thought of him daily and about his safety.

Kyle talked to Kashara frequently. He visited her regularly. I later found out he told his sister how he often felt that somebody was after him. He would cross the street or drive a different route to avoid them.

 I remember he had his first paranoid-like episode when he was nineteen. He called 2 a.m. one morning and said somebody was following him with a gun. He said he wasn't sure if somebody was trying to set him up. He sounded very scared. I asked him to tell me where he was, and I would pick him up. I started praying in the spirit that he would be okay until I got to him. I was a little anxious until I found him. I drove around in the middle of the night looking for him and calling his cell phone until I found him. I wasn't familiar with the area, but I was praying. No matter what, a mother will see about her children to make sure that they are okay. When I got to where Kyle was, he came out of a gas station. He was looking behind to make sure nobody was following him.

He got in the car and was very anxious. He said, "Mom, they kept hiding behind buildings so I couldn't see their faces while I was walking. So, I went in the store of the gas station to hide." This was very real to him. He looked out of the window of the car and said, "I just saw them again, behind that building."

I looked, but I didn't see anyone. I drove back home. He said,

"Thank you, mom, for coming to pick me up because these people are crazy."

I asked him if he knew who was after him and he said,

"I don't know, and I couldn't see." He was still very anxious. He kept saying, "I think somebody is trying to set me up."

Kyle started to relax the closer we got to home. At this time he was dating Natasha, who also was called Tasha, not the young lady he took to the prom, but she was a young lady he grew up with in church. He thought it might have been Tasha's family trying to get him. I began to frown and asked why?

He said, "Because they don't like me. She has a

brother and I think he's in a gang and he might be after me."

This was the first time I heard that Tasha had a brother. I later questioned Tasha and told her what happen and asked her about this brother. At first, she didn't know who Kyle was talking about. Then she said he must be talking about her father's son. She said she hadn't seen him in a couple of years because he had gotten into some trouble and was incarcerated. She said that Kyle never met him, but he must have heard her family talking about him.

I just meditated on what he said. I could see his mind was racing so I changed the subject and started talking about his job and things that would relax him more. When we got home, I laid hands on him and prayed, and he seemed more settled. It was probably about 4 a.m. I knew that later in the morning, he would have to go to work, so I mentioned he should get some real rest. He then went upstairs and slept in his bedroom. Later, when he woke up, he seemed to be back to himself, talking with his father, brothers, and sisters. I later took him to work. Thinking about that night kept me in a riddle.

About a month after that incident, Kyle and I

were talking on the phone. He shared his frustration of what happened to his car. Kyle had a big heart and was a nice guy and people took advantage of that. One time, one of his, "so-called" friends was racing with his car and messed up his engine and transmission.

He said, "Mom, you were right about these people out here. They pretend to be your friends and use you."

He sounded truly angry. He told me someone stole his money and other things. I suggested that he could move back home if he wanted to. I ministered to him about God and how Jesus is forgiving. We all make mistakes at times. I mentioned to him that he needed to come back to the fellowship with the Lord and return to church.

So, he moved back home for a couple of months and went back to church. He didn't physically go to the altar, but he was back in fellowship with God and the church, and we were ecstatic. I've learned that we shouldn't push too much because we have to let God do the work and undo the damage.

When he returned home, he was able to start

back at True Green doing landscape work, which he loved.

He was increasingly dating his girlfriend. Natasha, who was affectionately named. Tasha is the girl who would later become his wife.

 Kyle's story resembled his dad's and my story about meeting his future "forever" in church, and growing up together.

Kashara told me that Tasha had a crush on Kyle for years and they'd been friends for years.

She said, "Mom, remember when Tasha gave her testimony that a man tried to rape her outside her building, and something happened that scared the man off? When Kyle found out, he was angry and went out looking for the man to beat him up." I said to myself, "Lord is this the Tasha you were talking about?" I smiled.

The Lord had revealed to me that Kyle's wife's name would be Tasha. Kyle dated two girls named Tasha who both went to church but the first Tasha he took to the prom, I could not see these two married because they were always passionately bickering with each other about something.

When our son was in search for a wife, there were certain guides and qualities to look for. For one, make sure she loves God. Looks aren't everything. Beauty is in the eyes of the beholder, so beauty should be on the inside as well as the outside. I taught him to set goals and to make sure her goals agree with his, and make sure you love her through everything, and she loves you back with the same intensity. Share the load of friendship and courtship.

I knew how hard he worked. There are women who just want to look beautiful and let their husbands do all the work. When I realized it was Tasha from our church, I was at ease.

I didn't let Kyle and Tasha know what God had told me until they were engaged. I just confirmed it. Natasha is a beautiful young lady, inside and out, and she is a church girl. I knew that she would take particularly good care of my son, and knowing my son, he would take great care of Tasha.

From the day he wanted to defend her from a rapist, was probably the day he was smitten. He wanted to be her protector, yet with her, it was she who protected him. It was he who felt safe.

Kyle and Tasha became engaged in March 2007. Of course, he was Tasha's knight in shining armor. What a birthday present for Tasha, a day before her birthday to have a life-changing event like becoming engaged. Feeling good and nervous about this new endeavor, he came by to show us the ring he selected for his bride to be. The rings were stunning. I surmised that he wanted that parental support from us before the proposal.

We all saw this gleam in his eyes and a beautiful smile on his face as he shared his joyful heart. He felt he had finally met the wife God had for him (his soulmate).

Genesis 2:24 *"Therefore shall a man leave his father and his mother, and shall cleave unto his wife: and they shall be one flesh,"*

The Bible also says when a man finds a wife he finds a good thing. The family was happy for Kyle. We knew that he loved Natasha intentionally. I think no one has ever heard him talk about a young lady so much before. She made him smile, and that was a good thing. Remember he was on the quiet side, but not when it came to Natasha because she was his happy place.

Along with the proposal, they became roommates at her place.

Tasha called me crying once, thinking she was going to lose her fiancé after having a dispute. She had his heart, I believed, and I let her know that. All mothers know their children. I told her not to worry, it would work itself out. I encouraged her to pray. Sure enough, they were able to work it out and proceed with the plans for their wedding.

This was a happy time in Kyle's life because things were going well for him. He bought himself a truck for his landscaping business, which was going well. He had two jobs because landscaping is seasonal. He eventually ended up with two trucks for his landscape business. He loved being a boss, having his own route and schedule. He enjoyed working alone and have his own space. He was still at True Green, going to church, and had the woman of his dreams in his life. Life was good for Kyle.

 While Kyle was going to church, he had not rededicated his life to the Lord. He was still doing his own thing like shacking, drinking, and using marijuana. Even though I didn't agree with his lifestyle, I was so glad he was in a place where he could be brought back to the things that nurtured him as a young boy in church.

Kyle came home from work one evening and he and Natasha got into a dispute. Kyle did have a fiery temper. His day was dreadful and frustrating at work. One of the neighbors called the police and said they were physically fighting. Due to the way the two-family house was made, the police were able to walk straight into the bedroom. The Police said someone called in a domestic violence incident. Tasha was just getting out of the shower at this time. Kyle opened the door partially, agitated that someone had called the police. There were two police officers. He asked the officers if they would wait until Tasha got dressed. He mentioned to them that she had just got out of the shower. The two officers were leaning on the door, so Kyle pushed the door closed. When he pushed the door closed, the police got agitated and kicked the door open and grabbed him, slammed him to the ground and cuffed him. He was wiggling and angry because it happened so suddenly.

Kyle had never been in trouble before with the police, so this was new to him. They cuffed him and all of a sudden more officers rushed into the bedroom. They began to beat him with the Billy club, hitting him in the head, face, back, and so forth. Tasha was standing there, terrified at how they were beating him. She panicked because she thought they were going to kill him. She walked toward her fiancé and the police and told them to stop beating him like that. One officer hit Natasha and told her to get back. When Kyle saw them hit Natasha, that made him go into a rage and move even more, while handcuffed. I'm sure he was trying to defend Tasha, but they beat him even more.

 Later, I found out there were about thirteen police officers in the house when it was over. Kyle told me that they put a gun to his head and said if he kept moving, they were going to shoot him. There were officers holding him down while others were beating him. They ended up arresting both my son and Natasha. If it was real domestic violence, they were supposed to protect the abused, not abuse and arrest them. Kyle was still living in Massachusetts at this time. After she was released, Tasha called me, from the police station, and told me what happened. I was outraged when I found out. Kyle was still locked up. I was not happy at all. The thought still upsets me, but I'm mentioning this for a reason. I told my husband what happened, and I went down to the police station. I was scared and nervous for my son, but I was praying for him. It is important to pray when you don't know what else to do because even though we are upset and angry, we still have to use wisdom and do things the right way.

Tasha's mom, Vanessa, was there with her when I got there. I asked to speak to the police because I wanted to make a complaint. I was in one of my adamant moods, so I did talk to the Captain, but didn't get too far. He told me how I could make a complaint and what the procedure was. When they finally released Kyle that night, I saw how badly they had beaten him, and I was even more upset. His face was all swollen and he had cuts by his eye and lumps in his head. He was bruised and battered all over his upper body.

Tasha said he was urinating blood but didn't want to go to the doctor. When I saw him, I asked him if he was all right, but Kyle, being the typical tough male, said he was okay. He was angry and frustrated about how they assaulted him. I was upset, enough to take legal action against the whole police department.

He was irate and did meet with a couple of

lawyers who didn't want to get involved. I eventually let the idea of suing the police department go because the Holy Spirit told me to leave it alone. Jesus can fight the battle better than we can.

Of course, the police were totally innocent in this situation, according to their standards. They accused Kyle of assault and battery with a weapon and stated that he used the door as a weapon (resisting arrest). They accused Tasha of assault because they said she tried to interfere with the arrest.

Due to this incident, Kyle ended up losing his job at True Green. It's amazing how you are prejudged due to pre conceived notions and the color of your skin. I always thought one was innocent until proven guilty. Kyle tried to fight the charges, but they told him if he fought it, he may end up doing jail time. So, he ended up settling and doing probation for a year. Natasha ended up settling, also, and doing probation for six months.

I mentioned this incident for a reason because it will be important later, relating to Kyle's death. Sometimes God allows things to happen for a reason because it's in His divine plan. We may never understand the various woes, tests, and trials, but we will understand later, as time passes.

Kyle, I believe never got over how the police mistreated him, but was resilient enough to bounced back. He continued to do his landscaping business and God blessed his business and grew his clientele.

CHAPTER 4

Marriage and Disruption

Kyle and Natasha married six months after their engagement. Some folk were of the opinion that he was too young to have a wife. He was 21. There were others who thought Kyle was a very responsible young man.

Not that it matters, but there was a three year difference between those two with Natasha being the older. They were already living together, and Kyle always wanted to do the right thing. They both loved each other, and other people's opinions didn't matter. The parents didn't have a problem with their marriage.

The night before the ceremony, his friends took him out for his bachelor's party, and he took his brother Kevin with him.

They wedded the next day at 10 a.m. September 15, 2007. It was a beautifully brisk and sunny Saturday morning.

I believe this was one of the happiest days of his

life. He was smiling from ear to ear, just beaming. He had some of his childhood friends in the wedding. Jeremy was his best man, Joey, Cody, and Joe were his groomsmen. All his siblings were in his wedding. Kevin and Keenan were his groomsmen, and Kashara and Kayla were bridesmaids. Their colors were white and baby blue. Kyle stayed at our house the night before the wedding due to the tradition; it was bad luck for the groom to see the bride before the wedding.

He looked incredibly handsome in the white tuxedo. He was a little nervous the morning of the wedding. He paced and paced. His father was talking to him to keep him occupied, then took him for a drive to keep him calm. Tasha's nephew, Noah, was the ring bearer, Jasalin, and Tayana, her nieces, were the beautiful flower girls.

Natasha was a gorgeous bride in her white wedding gown. She was escorted in a long stretch Hummer limousine and the married couple left in the same.

These were the nieces and nephews that Kyle was around a lot and grew fond of and loved. He played with them a lot and was very relaxed around them. They belonged to Tasha's sister,

Danielle, who they called Danny for short. Danny and Tasha are close sisters. Kyle loved children and told Tasha that he wanted them to have five of their own. Bertram and I were so proud of him. It was just a wonderful day. We were so happy for them. They went off after their wedding to a 10-day Caribbean cruise. They enjoyed themselves to the highest. They took many pictures. Kyle and Natasha had pictures made from the cruise and gave one set to each other's family. They made such a good couple and appeared so happy together. The newlyweds brought everyone gifts from their cruise. After settling in from their honeymoon excursion, newly husband began work at Yankee Candle.

Kyle and Natasha, the inseparable and romantic couple went everywhere together. They did shopping and laundry together, even before they got married. They were good together and good for each other. Kyle never forgot Tasha's birthday. He would send her flowers from time to time, not just on holidays, but just because. They often dined out, went to concerts, took day trips and went away for weekends. Kyle was a good husband, his father taught him well. He took loving care of Natasha. She was also an excellent wife to Kyle; she took particularly loving care of him. She cooked for him, not many young ladies know how to cook these days. She kept the house clean, did the laundry, the typical domestic chores. I'm not trying to be biased, but she reminded me of me. They always say that young men marry women like their mothers.   Tasha and I became very close after the wedding. She was very shy, at first, but we pulled her out of her shell. She is my third daughter; she calls me mom.

Kyle had a big heart towards people. Tasha told me if he saw someone on the road walking, he would offer them a ride, no matter how they looked. He would give pan handlers money or give friends money if they asked. If he saw someone in need, he would help in any way he could. When the Pastor needed help from the men, he would always volunteer if he knew about it. Unfortunately, there were people who took advantage of his kindness.

Sometime later, to support Tasha, Kyle agreed to take on joint responsibility to help out Tasha's sister, Danny, who was having some difficult family matters. The married couple took in Danny's son, Noah for a year. Noah was about six at the time. Kyle spent much time with Noah and provided him a father figure. He took Noah on family trips to Six Flags. They also enjoyed the excitement of Chucky Cheese, arcade games, and other social delights. Kyle and Tasha would even take their nieces sometimes, to give the grandmother a break. They all adored Kyle because he would play with them and give them a lot of attention. So, you know they must greatly miss Kyle.

Noah was just over recently. He comes over to play with Keenan. Once when I was driving him to the house, he was in the back seat talking to Keenan, just laughing. Noah is very smart, and he is very talkative at times. He repeated, "Uncle Kyle took me on a ride." He giggled on every memory of his uncle. I realized that our son left an indelible impression on Noah. Tasha says he constantly talks about Kyle. When the little one was once at the house, he sat on the couch and spoke about Kyle. He said he felt that his uncle is still with him, and pointed to his heart. I said to him, "He is with me in my heart too." That touched my heart deeply.

I know that he will never forget Kyle. The good values Kyle instilled in him will always be with him as he grows up. Noah loved Kyle.

Noah is the oldest child of his siblings and he's

been through challenging times. Noah used to be hyperactive, but when Kyle came into his life and spent much needed time with him, he calmed down a lot. Only men can mentor boys and teach them how to be men. So, all those happy memories Kyle left with Noah will over power the negative ones.

The married couple headed into 2008 with a hurdle. Not married a year, their love would be tested. There were some struggles. When he spoke on the issues, it was duly about the frustrations with his job at **Yankee Candle**. He thought they were trying to set him up and get rid of him. One female manager was micromanaging his every move, and just giving him a hard time.

Thinking back, knowing what I know now, I think those might have been signs of his paranoia spiraling out of control. He masked it well. He might have suppressed it through drinking and the use of drugs. He was a closet user of drugs and alcohol. We never knew our son drank until the last two years of his life. There was never a hint of drinking on his breath, but that could've been due to the respect he had for his mom and dad.

He never smoked or drank around me; however

he told me he had a smoking problem and was trying to quit the last year of his life.

Tasha confessed after his death, that he always drank, but tried cutting back after marriage. Kyle was proud to report that he was seven weeks sober. This was just before he died. Kyle was the serious closet drinker. He was dealing with issues in his mind like frustration and anger. He wanted to be normal or good, so he would just suppress his thoughts. When you deny yourself the freedom of being true to whomever you are, you are NOT your best self, and that's not good at all.

His gentle heart got him into careless and vulnerable situations at times and he got taken advantage of more than he cared to mention or let happen. He started backing off from people. Kyle wasn't trusting anyone except his family. He became a tormented soul because he was suppressing everything inside.

He perhaps was thinking of all the things that made him angry or flustered. He started having doubts and regrets about marriage.

Evil thoughts will bombard you when you are at your lowest point. When you become isolated from those who love and care for you, because of trailing thoughts, evilness will take you on a ride that you might not soon get off. I encouraged him to hang in there and pray. I told him that Jesus would fix it eventually by either moving people out of his way or blessing him with another job.

Kyle hung in a little while longer on his job at Yankee Candle, but eventually was laid off in June 2009.

I thought this was the best thing that could have happened because he was not happy at that job, and he struggled so much with the people there.

He once told me that one of the workers screamed in his face and was cursing and calling him names, trying to start a fight. The police were called. Kyle and the other worker got written up. He didn't fight back because he didn't want to lose his job. I just told him to pray and tell the truth and it would work out. The other worker eventually ended up getting fired. God always takes care of His people and prayer does change things! They didn't even want to pay Kyle unemployment. He always had Tasha write down everything that happened and kept all his paperwork, which was good. He went to court and finally got his unemployment benefits. Thank

God!

Things went on the decline rapidly for Tasha and Kyle. Landscaping was not going well for him due to the state of the economy at the time and people were careful how they spent their money. Unfortunately, when President Obama was elected in 2008, he inherited an economy that was in great jeopardy.

June 2009, jobs were even more hard to find. Kyle was usually a very busy person, so with no job and landscaping slow, things were tough, which caused more frustration in the newest dynamic; their marriage. I heard from Kyle less because his cell phone was frequently broken or not working. When I called Tasha's phone, she would say they were o.k. but I could hear the disparity in her voice. Almost every time, I would ask about Kyle, she would say, his phone was broken or lost again. I think he was breaking his phone out of frustration. **Kyle began to isolate himself increasingly.**

CHAPTER 5

Death All In The Family

Deaths were ramped and plenteous on my side of the family in 2009. We lost three family members that year. The first person we lost was my uncle, Bishop Napoleon. He was like a father to me. He was my father's youngest brother.

 My maternal mother had nine children, of which I was child number six. Both our parents died young. We were initially sent to foster care. My Uncle Napoleon lived in Holyoke, Mass. He and his wife, Louise, could not have children. In his wife's failed attempt to bare children from miscarriage after miscarriage, the last attempt, almost killed her, so she had to have a total hysterectomy at an early age. They became parents to six of us and I was the youngest of the six. My uncle would later die sadly on March 14th, 2009, of cancer. That was like losing my dad all over again. Kyle was very close to my uncle, who was like a grandfather to him, he would go by and check in on him as he got older. My uncle was a barber for over 40 years and cut Kyle's hair when he was younger.

 The second death was Eugenia, my sister-in-law. She did a lot of evangelistic work. She was the most bold and courageous woman of God I'd ever met. She mentored me well when I became an evangelist.

Eugenia worked so hard but was in denial she had diabetes the last 15 years of her life and was not in compliance with the disease.   The last six months of her life, she ended up going into kidney failure. She was a courageous woman. She would counsel and encourage other women in God's word. This was Aunt Geanna to Kyle; she ran a very successful daycare center for 13 years and Kyle worked for her during his early teens helping to clean the daycare toys. Eugenia would encourage Kyle spiritually and naturally. She loved, adored Kyle and use to say he was her favorite nephew. Aunt Geanna told Kyle how handsome he was, and he would be grinning and blushing. She sadly died July 2nd, 2009.

The third death was my Aunt Annie, my father's second oldest sister. She was a strong, courageous woman of God. My Aunt Annie was a wise and a powerful prayer warrior. She might have prayed for 100,000 or more people in her lifetime. She prayed for people all over the country, especially families. Aunt Annie's health began to decline when she was about 76 years old. She developed a blood clot in her leg. Later, she was diagnosed with leukemia and had to go through chemotherapy. She lived about seven more years before the leukemia came back. Kyle would help his Great Aunt Annie with her yard work when she first got sick. Aunt Annie went home to be with the Lord on Thursday October 8th, 2009.

Losing all those loved ones took a toll on my entire family.

86
Enrico Fermi High School
Enfield   Connecticut
This Certifies That
Kyle Christopher Edwin Robinson
has completed the prescribed Course of Study and is therefore awarded this
Diploma
as a certificate of graduation from Enrico Fermi High School
Given at Enfield, in the State of Connecticut,
June, 2004.
Chairperson of Board of Education
Secretary of Board of Education
Principal
Superintendent of Schools
PLAINS SCHOOL
FOSTER SCHOOL
MRS REDMAN
GRADE 2

1995 STEFANIK MEMORIAL 1996
SCHOOL
DOWN TO GO

CHAPTER 6

Preparing For The Future

Since the lay-off in June, Kyle had more time on his hands. I was doing an outreach revival at the Holiday Inn hotel near the end of June. This was my second revival at the Holiday Inn hotel since establishing the Holy Ghost Temple Prayer and Deliverance Radio and Outreach Ministry in 2007. Kyle came to support us on Saturday of the revival. All our children Tasha, Kashara, Keenan, and Kayla were the praise team, under the direction of Kevin. My drummer didn't show up that night so Kyle played the drums. Kashara was the videographer for the services which a lot of them are on YouTube.

We started to see a new change in Kyle after all the deaths in our family. He was going to church more and getting more involved in the services. One day, in late October 2009, I was preaching a message on Spiritual Warfare. I called a prayer line for all the people struggling with spiritual warfare and Kyle was one of the people who came up for prayer. Prayer was rendered for all who were dealing with the evil spirits they were warring with. The Holy Spirit fell on Kyle, and he started to leap. This video is also on YouTube with him leaping under prophetic flow. Kyle often leaped when the Holy Spirit would fall on him.

Six weeks before Kyle was killed, he called me on a Tuesday morning and began to tell me it was time for him to get his life right with God because time was short. I was happy to hear this because I had been praying for this day. He said, "I'd been fasting today so I can go down to the altar tonight." Tuesday night was tarrying service at our church. He told me he had stopped drinking and smoking one week prior to this Tuesday. He said, "Mom, I called so you can say the sinner's prayer with me before I go down to the altar, because I want to get it right." He was seriously hungry for change. I read with him from the book of **Romans (10:9-10)**, *"That if thou shalt confess with thy mouth the Lord Jesus, and shalt believe in thine heart that God hath raised him from the dead, thou shalt be saved. For with the heart man believeth unto righteousness and with the mouth confession is made unto salvation."*

First we have to admit that we are sinners in

order to be saved. Then we must ask Jesus for forgiveness in faith, and He will forgive us completely, therefore giving us a new start. However, we cannot leave out forgiveness of ourselves. This is vital. God will forgive, other people can forgive you, but if you are unable to forgive yourself, you can never be in peace with yourself or free in the mind. Kyle was reading right along with me. Once we were done, he seemed relieved. I talked with him a little longer, encouraging and praying with him. I told him I would see him at church.

Sure enough, he was there that Tuesday night, and as soon as the altar was open, he went down and began calling on Jesus' name.

Romans 10:13 says, *"For whosoever shall call upon the name of the Lord shall be saved."*

I came down from the pulpit to pray with him. I anointed his head with olive oil and prayed that God would pull his mind in, and touch every thought process. I could see he was struggling. I told him that Jesus loves him and how much of a loving Savior Jesus is, along with that, he needed the gumption to forgive himself because Jesus had already done so. Then his tears flooded his face as he continued to call Jesus. I saw just how much emotional pain my son was in. I saw all the frustration in his face. I could see the enemy was tormenting him about the mistakes he had made; flashing them through his mind. As his tears streamed down his face, like oceans of pain, I could tell he was still having a hard time forgiving himself.

When Kyle got up from the altar, I complimented him that he did good. I encouraged him to keep tarrying because he needed to release more things from his spirit, soul, and body. One of the first things was to forgive himself. I kept reiterating, "Jesus loves you. Through Jesus' love, we are made perfect." Whatever he did in that first year he left the church, had him bound, and he needed to be released from that.

The enemy was not happy that he had gone down to the altar. Friday came around and an evil spirit had attacked Kyle's mind again with another paranoid episode. This was the second time I visually witnessed Kyle in paranoia, and this was a severe case.

It was a Friday night, and he was at the church doing the landscaping. Tasha was the breadwinner for the family since Kyle was not seriously working. Both trucks were broken, and there wasn't enough money to fix them. He did keep the grounds of the church.

I believe he took the bus from Springfield to West Springfield to the church that day. I had some errands to run, and when I got home, Kyle was sitting at the table. His dad and I were supposed to go on a date that evening. I went in the bedroom and Bertrum said to me that Kyle's conversation was he thought somebody was out to get him. I went back into the kitchen, he looked very tensed and anxious. I sat at the table with him and said,

"Your father mentioned to me that you think someone is after you. He looked at me and said,

"Mom, they thought they had me, but I out smarted them. I was working outside at the church, and something told me that they were going to try to set me up to kill me in the driveway. I think that it's Tasha's family, so I left and caught the bus home, and they were all looking at me (at the bus stop); and I know they were talking about me. They were planning to shoot me in the driveway."

He was tapping his fingers on the table anxiously.

He said, "So I rushed home and called a taxi to bring me over here."

I asked him why he didn't call me because I would have picked him up. He said,

"I didn't want them to follow me, so I took a cab. I think Tasha is in on it also."

I frowned and said,

"Tasha would never hurt you because she loves you very much."

I let him know that he was safe now, and I'm always praying **Exodus 12:13ᵃ** over him, a covering of the blood on him so no one could harm him.

And the blood shall be to you for a token upon the houses where ye are: and when I see the blood, I will pass over you,

He looked in my eyes and said,

"I know mom, they said that's why I am still alive all this time, because of your prayers."

I asked him why he thought Tasha's family was after him. He looked down, paused a little, and said,

"Well I picked up this lady one night because she wanted me to do some landscaping for her. I took her out to dinner a couple of times, but I never slept with her. She was a crack head anyway."

I asked him if he told Tasha about it. He said,

"I did, but I think she has not forgiven me for it."

"We all make mistakes in life, and as long as you were honest with Tasha, she would forgive you." I uttered.

This is something they needed to talk about. It's hard to feel betrayal, but I knew how much Tasha loved him. It would take work, but I felt this issue could heal, and they could get back to loving each other wholly again. However, I could tell that he couldn't forgive himself, or didn't know how. He was struggling so much.

I said to him he did well by going down to the altar. He got up from the table and started pacing. I knew he needed some time so I told him he could stay at our house as long as he needed to. He sat on the floor in the living room in front of the couch. He grabbed the Bible off the end of the table. His mind, preoccupied.

He began flipping through the Bible. He said,

"Mom I don't have much time. I know I need to get my life right, so when my time comes, I will be ready."

I pondered on what he said, like Mary, the mother of Jesus, pondered on the words Jesus spoke in her heart.

He started to get anxious again and was looking around. I asked him where Tasha was and he said,

"I don't know, I think she is still at work."

Tasha worked until 6:30 p.m. and it was about 6:00 p.m. at the time. I said,

"Why don't you just give her a call, so she won't be worried about you and let her know that you are over here."

He took his phone out from his pocket and reassembled it. He pulled the battery out so he wouldn't get any calls. He then called Tasha but she didn't pick up, so he left a message. The call came in, it was Tasha calling back.

His voice was a little hostile when he said to her, "I am over my mom's house." He talked a little more, but said he would call her later.

I was just happy he called her so she wouldn't worry. Then, he disassembled his phone again by taking the battery out. Suddenly, he jumped up and said,

"I am going to get me something to eat."

He put the Bible down on the floor. I offered to drive him because he had no vehicle. It was drizzling, damp, and cold because it was the second week in November. He said,

"No mom, I'll just ask Kashara if I can use her bike."

I asked if he was coming back and he said yes, he was just going to get something to eat.

"Make sure you call one of us. Your father and I are going out to eat, but wouldn't be gone that long."

Then he asked Kashara to use her bike. He never made it back. It was my plan to pray for him when he got back. I don't know why I didn't do it before he left. All I know is that during that time, it was important for me to listen to him. I tried reaching out to him on his phone, but he didn't pick up. It went straight to voicemail. It might have been disassembled still. I called Tasha the next day to see if he had returned to her. She answered no.

"No? What?" I was in utter shock over her answer. I just knew he would be home since he didn't return to us. I gave her the story Kyle rehearsed to us about her family being after him. She seemed puzzled. She was emphatic that her family was not after him. She confided that sometimes Kyle would stay away for a day or so if he needed space. His practice would be to call her and come home.

She knew I would be praying and would let me know when she'd hear from him. I called back once again to see if he had returned. The answer was still no, but she heard from him, and was asked to pick up the check from the church for the landscaping he did. He would call later. Needless to say, for him not to go home, this gave me great pause.

Tasha came to church on the following Sunday. Again, she hadn't heard from him, and she sounded nervous and concerned.

"Had he ever stayed away this long?"

"No."

Monday and Tuesday went by, and no sign of Kyle. The whole family was concerned and praying. Tuesday night, we continued with our prayer and tarrying service, still utterly and genuinely concerned. We asked the Lord to let us know where he was and to let him be all right.

Natasha was very worried and scared. I told her to continue to pray. Late Tuesday night, about 11 p.m., Kashara was checking her messages on the cell phone. She came running frantically into my room. There was a message left on her cell phone to call Hartford Hospital. It was about Kyle.

"You call, mom." Although I was lying down, I jumped up, relieved yet a little anxious. I was praising God because, at least we knew where he was.

I called the number to the Hartford emergency room. When the nurse answered, I told her my daughter received a message to call about Kyle Robinson. She explained that Kyle would not give any information about his family, so checking his clothes, we found a Kashara's phone number on a piece of paper in his pocket. She revealed that Kyle was okay physically, but very anxious. He was sure somebody was out to get him. The nurse mentioned that Kyle told the Windsor Police he was hiding out in a hotel because somebody was out to kill him. He called the police for a ride to the airport, so he could get a flight to Washington, D.C. He had to hide in a shelter so no one could find him. The police, in turn brought him to the hospital.

 I asked if I could speak to him.

"We gave him a sedative to relax him."

I wanted him to know it was his mother on the line. They got him the phone. When he picked up he said,

"Hi mom."

He had to know how worried we were because we hadn't heard from him.

"Kyle, are you alright?"

He said yes.

"I'm coming to see you."

He quickly told me he didn't want to see anybody because he didn't want anyone to see him like that. Gingerly, I asked to let me come and visit so I could ease my heart. I didn't push the issue of anyone else, even Tasha. He replied,

"Okay mom, just you."

He sounded flat and very drowsy.

I recapped "I love you and make sure you call me."

 We hung up. I talked back to the nurse, and she said they were going to keep him in the mental health facility for a little while longer due to paranoia. The whole family was relieved to find out where he was and to know he was okay, especially his wife.

CHAPTER 7

The Discovery

Kyle was in the hospital for one week. Thank God he was physically okay. That was a very scary time for everyone. I visited him in the hospital a few times. I talked with him and prayed with him on the phone every day. The first time I went to see him, I went by myself because he didn't want to see anybody else. He looked very down and tired. I hugged him, and he said,

"Hi mom."

His mind was still very preoccupied. We went to a private room to visit. In the room, there was a little table with chairs, so we sat at the table. I asked him how he was really doing, and he said okay. They were giving him medications to relax him and help him sleep.

I asked how did he get to Windsor and he answered that he rode Kashara's bike to the Windsor Library and locked it up.

"Tell Kashara her bike was okay because I

secured it. No one should steal it because I put it in a safe place. I know that area well."

When he worked for True Green, he would have to drive in a lot of different areas in Connecticut, so he got to know lots of locations. I comforted him by letting him know that the bike wasn't important, and not to worry about it. Kashara can always get another bike. I said,

"We are just happy that you are okay."

He was still genuinely concerned about the bike and talked about it a little more.

He said,

"When I went in the library, mom, there were about ninety people in there (his voice elevated as he began to talk). They were all staring at me, they were all talking about how they were planning to kill me. They were whispering about how they were going to kill me and put me in a trunk of a car."

I just listened to him. He spewed more,

"Mom can you believe there were ninety people in that library? Wow! I left when they weren't looking."

He paused again, then he said,

"I know it sounds crazy."

He looked at me and gave me a half grin. I knew this was very real to him. He said,

"Maybe it's all in my head. Maybe these meds they have me on will help me."

We continued to talk a little while longer. I encouraged him and let him know that God was going to work it out.

"You are in a good place so you can talk out all these feelings with the doctors."

He grinned again and said,

"Yeah, they think I'm crazy!"

He relaxed even more. I asked if he had called his wife, and he said no because he wasn't sure she would understand. I assured him that Tasha loved him and was sure she would be willing to listen.

"Just be honest with her and both of you will be able to work through it."

Before I left, I prayed with him, and we hugged. I told him I loved him, and he said,

"I love you too, Mom."

While in the psych hospital, Kyle was evaluated and was diagnosed with paranoid schizophrenia. The doctors prescribed Haldol, Depakote and Cogentin, which are antipsychotic drugs and mood stabilizers. Psychosis is when you hear voices and see things other people don't see. We, in the spiritual realm, call them demonic spirits. The medications are heavy sedatives that slow down the brain activity and subdues it so that those thoughts are suppressed. We know when people see these spirits and illusions they are very real to them and if they are not able to pull their minds back, these thoughts and illusions can be very terrifying. That's why prayer is especially important to help us control our thoughts and concentrate on spiritual things, so our minds don't wander too far.

If the devil knows he can instill fear in you with irrational thoughts, he will continue to torment you. He preys on your fears and weaknesses. If he knows your fear is death, he will continue to bring thoughts of death to terrify you. 2nd **Timothy 1:7 "For God hath not given us the spirit of fear, but of power, and of love, and of a sound mind."**

We can't stop the thoughts from coming, but we can certainly cast them down, and substitute those thoughts with another thought; such as a prayer, a scripture, or an affirmation.

I took a Bible when I went to visit him, and gave him some scriptures to read; **Philippians 3:8-16 and 2nd Timothy 1:7**, so he could forget about his past mistakes and move on. I also gave him these scriptures so at any time he felt anxious, he could read them out loud. I wanted him to memorize these scriptures so he could speak to them and put the *devil* and *fear* in their place. The devil doesn't like when we speak God's Word because it accomplishes what God destined it to do. Fear will have to leave, and calm will settle in your spirit. The third scripture was **Ephesians 6:10-18,** which describes putting on the whole armor of God because we wrestle not against flesh and blood, but spiritual wickedness in high places (Satan's devices). We need to put on our spiritual armor to fight against Satan's attacks. I knew these three scriptures would help build him up spiritually against Satan's attacks in his mind, and decrease that paranoia. I told him to read the scriptures every day so they would be planted in his spirit.

I called the next day, asking him if he were soaking in the scriptures and he said yes. I wondered if he felt better, and he said yes. I admonished that he continue doing these rituals by force, habit, until it was like first nature as to keep his mind filled with the word of God.

When I went for another visit, I took my brother, Pastor Leroy. I confided in him about Kyle. He told me the next time; he would go with me to talk and pray with his nephew.

Our pastors are our spiritual coverings. God put them as watchman over our souls, so they can see in the spiritual realm, what is going on, and serve as protectors for our souls. This is called spiritual discernment.

When we got there, Kyle was happy to see his uncle. Pastor Leroy gave Kyle a big hug. We were able to use the private room for our visit. Kyle opened up to his uncle by saying,

"Sometimes, I get so angry. I don't know why I am so angry all the time."

I remember him telling me, on the first visit, about all the people in the Library whom he thought were after him.

He said to me, "You know I am not afraid of them at all, Mom, but I am afraid of me and what I might do!"

Pastor Leroy told his nephew that it was important to talk out things on his mind, and not let them be held inside his mind. He told him to talk to his wife, his mother, or he could even come and talk to him.

It seemed now like more than just a mention, but a mandatory request that Kyle come to his uncle's office for conversations with him.

While in discussion of their visit, Kyle told him about some of the mistakes he'd made in his life. Pastor Leroy said,

"We all have made mistakes in our lives, but we just ask God for forgiveness, and we go on."

"Kyle, forgive yourself and let it go!" I exclaimed.

We talked a while longer. Pastor Leroy encouraged him to keep praying and reading his Bible. After Pastor prayed, we left. I sensed that Kyle felt much better after our visit because he seemed brighter, and his countenance was lifted.

These were challenging times for Tasha because

Kyle still had not called her, so I kept her abreast of things going on with her husband.

It wasn't important that I know their conversations because I'm not an intrusive mother-in-law. But if important conversations are not had or situations ignored, the wedge will get larger and larger between them. Secrets need to be brought in the open, so the devil won't have the power of torment over you and hold them as weapons against you. He'll give you high anxiety about it. However, if you bring them out in the open, then you can deal with them and release them. This is therapy by itself and emotional healing. Toward the end of their stay, he notified me that he finally called his wife, and they were talking.

The third time I visited was on a Sunday after church, and I brought Kashara and Kevin with me. Kyle was much more centered, but still brought up the concerns about Kashara's bike. He told her where it was and that it was locked up, and that he would get it when he got out of the hospital. Kashara told him not to worry about it. We talked some more, and his siblings had him laughing and smiling.

Kyle was released the Wednesday before

Thanksgiving. Due to no medical insurance because of unemployment, he went home with a starter kit of a two-week supply of medication, and he had just enough money to pay for it. His doctors were supposed to set him up with the local mental health facility so he could continue to get his medication.

Now Kyle had never taken medication in his life. I always prayed over my children and God healed them.

The medication made him feel really drowsy. They scheduled him an appointment for December 16. Kyle spent one week with the family before going back home. That was a blessing, knowing what I know now.

He spent Thanksgiving with us, but I could tell he missed his wife. After we ate, we gave him use of the car to go to Tasha. His face lit up like the fourth of July. He asked if I were sure. When I replied with a resounding yes, he disappeared for the rest of the evening to be with his Tasha. In his consideration, he wanted to make sure no one would need the car and of course, we didn't.

"Stay as late as you desire."

He mentioned that he and Tasha were rebuilding, and I was happy about that. He got in home late that night.

During that week, at our home, it was like old times. I got up early every morning and he would get up too. Kyle was an early riser. He and I just talked. He appeared to be coming back to himself. When he got up, he took his meds, and we discussed a prescription schedule. A couple of medications were twice a day, and the other one was three times a day.

While he stayed with us, he bought a vehicle from our good friend, Lucas, who was our mechanic. The vehicle was a 1996, red Chevy Corsica. The mechanic sold it to him for a decent price. His wife drove the car for years, even after his death.

 Kyle and Tasha talked several times a day. They were rebuilding their relationship as well as Kyle with his dad and all his brothers and sisters while home.

The following Tuesday, he went back to the altar again, and I could see the Holy Ghost all over him. He had a glow on his face when he got up. By the end of the week he was back with his wife, where he belonged. He was also going to church consistently, on Sundays, Tuesdays, and Thursdays. He went back down to the altar the next service. He was making his amends with God. One Sunday after church, I was talking to him in the hall and asked him how he was doing. He said, happily, he was doing well. He said, "Tasha and I have been reading the Bible together and praying." Then he told me he was reading Bishop T.D. Jakes' book on how to be a godly man. He said it was an enjoyable book. He was so happy and at peace.

The Friday before his death, he took his wife out for dinner. Tasha confided in me of Kyle's confessions of many things, even some things that didn't pertain to their relationship. He wanted to be totally candid with her. He asked for forgiveness of which she did.

That Saturday, there was a winter concert at the church, December 12, 2009. I was the moderator for the program, so I was busy. Kyle and Tasha were there. I found out later that he was crying at the concert and went back to Pastor Leroy's office and was talking to him for a good 30 minutes, then the Pastor prayed for him.

After the concert, we all went to eat at a local pizza joint, where the church treated the choir.

All the Robinson children were there as a part of the choir.

My nephew, Minister Eugene, the choir director, said,

"Come on Auntie, we'll treat you too."

Kyle accompanied his wife because she was a choir member. They sat at the table across from me. He was a little quiet, but that wasn't unusual because he wasn't very talkative around a lot of people.

When we left, Kyle made sure I was okay and safe by walking me to my car because the ground was a little slippery. He waited until all his siblings got in the car okay, then he proceeded to his car where he and Tasha sat in their car. It was almost 12:30 a.m., but he wouldn't drive off until he saw us on the move. (the protector).

Tasha saw that Kyle wasn't doing well. He was throwing up. It might have been symptoms of withdrawals from the medication he was prescribed. The two weeks he was on these three prescriptions and never got anymore, may have been a problem. We felt that Kyle fell through the cracks. He didn't pursue the medicine issue because he wasn't used to taking meds anyway, and he claimed to be feeling better.

It had been two weeks since he had the medications. He was on high dosages of these pills for his condition. Antipsychotic drugs are potent and just can't be stopped abruptly. He continued throwing up Sunday morning. He could not hold any food down, but he wanted to go to church. Thus he pressed through his physical ailment and went anyway. He was sobbing after the message.

Kyle and Tasha came up for prayer and the Pastor prayed over them. Kyle was lining his life up with God. Tasha said he still didn't feel well, so they went home after church. He slept for the rest of the day. She said the day after, he still wasn't feeling well. He took her to work and stayed in the parking lot until lunchtime and they went to lunch together.

He was crying again because he didn't think she'd forgiven him. She tried reassuring him that her love was real therefore the forgiveness was real. Kyle wasn't the type to cry, he was a man's man, but God knows how to break down a man's heart and Kyle was making everything right with his wife. Sometime after lunch, he sent flowers to his wife on the job.

The same evening he picked her up at 6:30 p.m. and brought her to the women's meeting at the church and waited for her again. When the meeting was over, they were supposed to go shopping, but Kyle still didn't feel his best so they went home.

She made them supper, but he didn't eat much. He felt really hot and sweaty. In spite of his feelings, he decided to go for a little ride, and claimed he'd be back.

They prayed before he left. They grabbed hands. Kyle prayed first, proceeded by Tasha's prayer. They kissed, said the usual 'I love you' then he left.

That was the last time Tasha saw Kyle alive.

Sunday was our last time seeing Kyle after church. He had given himself a nice short haircut because he had worn long braids for years. He was dressed up in a nice suit, looking extremely handsome. I hugged him after church and told him I loved him and he said,

"I love you too, Mom." That's the last visual I have of him alive.

CHAPTER 8

The Last Tuesday

Tasha uncovered that the last four weeks of Kyle's life was the happiest she had ever seen him. He was more relaxed and more open. She said he was a changed man. When Kyle left out that evening he was wearing all black.

Tuesday morning about 8:30 a.m. Tasha, concerned, called and asked me if I had seen Kyle because he never came home the night before, of which he said he would.

"How was his mood?"

"He seemed calm."

Kyle never replaced his cell phone after that second paranoid episode, subsequently Tasha had no way of contacting him.

Tasha had to be at work by 10 a.m. I said to her,

"He knows you have to go to work, and I know he'll be there to take you to work."

Kyle is loving and responsible. I felt he would be there to make sure Tasha got to work.

"Call me when he gets back or if he doesn't come in time for you to go to work."

Before hanging up, we prayed that Kyle was ok. My hopeful spirit told me that he WAS OK, and I relayed that message to her.

When hearing that kind of implication in your heart, you don't readily get the idea that it could be eternal.

There are times when God is saying "he's ok", He is really talking about immortality and the Kingdom of Heaven. His plan is totally different than ours because he has taken him into eternity.

Of course, this caught me off guard because I thought Kyle was doing so well. I asked God in my spirit, again, if Kyle was okay and the spirit said yes. I then relinquished my worry, with a tiny thought of where was he and why hadn't he come home.

8 For my thoughts are not your thoughts, neither are your ways my ways, saith the Lord. 9 For as the heavens are higher than the earth, so are my ways higher than your ways, and my thoughts than your thoughts. **Isaiah 55:**

8-9

The night before, I worked a different shift than normal, second shift, which was supposed to be from 3:00 - 11:30 p.m. It was a most trying set of eight and a half hours; I think I've had in a long while. I didn't actually get off until about 1 a.m. Understand that in nursing, sometimes, you will be confronted with issues that prevents you from getting off at your normal time because you can't leave your job duties until everything's done, or you are relieved from your duties into the next shift.

When I woke up that Tuesday morning, I turned on the news, as usual, to see what was going on. I had to get my two youngest children, Kayla and Keenan, off to school. The news reported that 91 North was blocked off for hours because an unidentified man had been hit by a tractor trailer truck. I thought, wow, that's terrible. I didn't have time to watch because I was running late. After I got the kids off to school, I tried to lay back down because from the 1:00 a.m. shift end, I didn't get home until 2:30 a.m.

After dropping off the kids to school, I thought I'd call Tasha since Kyle was on my mind. It was around 10:00 in the morning. I had hoped he had come home.

Being that she had to be at work by 10 am, I surmised that all was well, as she didn't reach out to me.

I called her mobile phone, she picked up.

I rendered soft niceties as I asked,

"Are you at work?"

"No."

"Well, have you heard from Kyle?"

"No."

My heart dropped. She sounded scared, too.

"I will continue praying. Call the moment you hear anything."

In my heart of hearts, I am on high alert concerned. I'm trying to rationalize the moment. Kyle would never leave his wife stranded for work without calling.

Hanging up the phone, I asked nervously in my spirit, "Lord you said he's okay?" And again, the spirit said,

"Yes."

The Lord knows everything from the beginning. Absolutely, nothing is hidden from Him, nor does anything catch Him by surprise. God is Omni-present. God is Ubiquitous, being everywhere at the same time. God is Omniscient, knowing all things, so God knew exactly where Kyle was. Being human and in the spirit, It is hard to trust the process that life sets. I had no hand in the matter, I had to yield to the authority of life. I am now praying for my own soul. While praying, the Lord brought to me, the life insurance policy for Kyle.

I said, "Lord if you are flashing the life insurance before me that means that you took him? This is what you mean about him being okay because you took him?"

Six years before, the husband and I took out a life insurance coverage on all our children. The insurance agent offered us a policy for the whole family, Kyle was about seventeen at the time. The agent said most families don't think to get life insurance for children until they are older. He said it's better to have it and not need it, than to need it and not have it. So, my husband and I agreed to insure the children for a few extra dollars because you just never know. The plan coverage was for $10,000 per child, up to age 25.

After that revelation, it was impossible for me to lay down because my nervous energy took me over. Christmas was essentially two weeks away, so I decided to go Christmas shopping.

I didn't call my daughter-in-law about the encounter with the Lord, I continued praying,

"Lord let us know where he is."

I went to the Wal-Mart, around 2 p.m. While there, I get a call in from a frail, shaky, frightened, and frantic voice on the line. It is Tasha.

"Mom, the state police is at the door, and I just want you to be on the phone while they are talking."

"Okay sweetie, I'm here."

My heart was racing a million miles a minute, but my voice sounded calm.

The officer asked when was the last time she'd seen Kyle and she answered. The officer went on to say that they found Kyle's wallet not too far from a body that had been struck in the street. They weren't absolutely sure it was Kyle.

Wow, God asked me a question during my time with him. Insurance policy. Now I knew why. It was because the Lord had prepared me for this moment. The state trooper left and gave Tasha his card. On the way out the door, the officer said,

 "We will stay connected and let you know when we find out any more information."

After the state trooper left, I asked Tasha what other questions did he ask.

"He asked if Kyle lived there and what relation was she to him."

I asked that she keep me informed on any discoveries and to call if she needed anything from me.

When I hung up, I breathed from my spirit,

"Lord, I know if you took him, you took him for a reason. I know you are too wise to make a mistake. Lord, as long as I know he's in glory with you, I'm okay. I trust you with my life and my children's lives."

Now, I had to pull my fragile soul and body together because I had to call my husband to abreast him of what was going on.

Bertram seemed to answer on the first ring when he saw my number on his caller ID.

"Honey, are you home or driving?"

"I got off early so yes, I'm home."

"I have some not-so-good news. Tasha got a visitor earlier this morning from a state trooper saying they had found Kyle's wallet near a body that was struck on Hwy 91 North."

Bertrum's voice, normally strong and confident, weakened from the sound of my frail and shaking voice,

"Are they sure it was Kyle?"

"They are still investigating."

I interrupted Bertram's conversation to answer the call coming in.

"Honey, you can hold the line, or I can call you back. It's Tasha."

"Mom, they want me to go and identify the body. I need a ride."

"No problem, I'll be right over to get you."

I felt I needed to be strong and stay tough for Tasha, the children, and Bertram. So I dissolved myself into this super-human role, pushed my shopping cart to the register, paid for my purchase, and headed to Kyle and Tasha's house.

I called my husband back to let him know what was going on. He was at the house with the children.

Bertram said, " I called my brother, Veral, to let him know what was going on."

 I turned on the Christmas music so it would replace my thoughts while I was driving. I definitely needed Jesus to minister to my soul.

He will bear us up in our weakest hour. And If I'd ever needed strength, it was at that moment. I relied on the truth that He was carrying me.

When I got to Tasha's house, I called to let her know I was there. She told me the police called back and told her,

"Do not come."

While still in the driveway, she came out, and got in the car. With a pause in her countenance, Tasha told me the police called her three more times since I last talked to her. She said the body they found last night was hit by a tractor trailer on the highway. They said the man was running across the highway and was struck.

The officer said the body was unidentifiable, that's why they told her not to come. They asked her how tall was he, the color of his skin, his shoe size, and body build.

The medical examiner had his body for a couple of days before they released it because they wanted to make sure it was him. His body was so dismembered that there was only an arm and a part of a leg salvageable.

My mind flashed back to what I saw on the news earlier that morning. They were talking about Kyle. I knew the devil must have attacked his mind with an episode of paranoia again. Just brace yourself for what I am about to say next. This is a horrible, tragic death to the unbelievers and to some believers, too.

So I asked her to come home with us so she wouldn't be alone. I stopped by the church and asked her to come with me inside. That might sound strange, but where do Christians go when they don't know what else to do? We go to church because we draw strength from the altar and from one another.

There is a chorus of a song that says,

"Where could I go, seeking a refuge for my soul, needing a friend to save me in the end, where could I go, but to the LORD."

2nd Corinthians 5:8 *"We are confident, I say, and willing rather to be absent from the body, and to be present with the Lord."*

This body is just clay, and it is going back to the dust. We didn't come here to stay, so we just need to be ready when our time comes. Remember Kyle had lined his life up with God before his demise.

My husband had a lawyer look into Kyle's death to make sure the trucker wasn't at fault. It took an entire year to get the police report back. It came back the last week of November 2010. The attorney called to let us know the trucker was not at fault.

According to the police report, Kyle was trying to cross the highway. Remember he was dressed in all black. This was about 2 a.m. on that Tuesday morning and it was still very dark. Kyle had made it across the South bound lane on Interstate 91 South, and was trying to make it across the North bound lane. The trucker didn't see him until he was three feet in front of him. The trucker clipped him, but other vehicles ran over his body also. The trucker pulled over and called 911.

The positive side to this is, if they had never found Kyle's wallet next to his body, we would have never known what had happened to him. So, I thank God for all things. The unknown is more tormenting than the known. At least we were able to find closure. Some people never do.

They were able to positively identify Kyle by his finger prints. Remember when the police arrested him for domestic violence, (even though it was not true), and they beat him so violently? It was for such a time as this because if he had never been in any trouble prior or subsequent to that incident. It was all in God's divine plan.

I started back to the house with Tasha. At this point, the police are in search for Kyle's car.

My husband told the children what was going on. They all hugged Tasha. Kashara asked anxiously if we found out any more information and I told her what was found out.

Kayla came down and asked what happened to Kyle, she had just awaken.

Kayla told me she had just had a dream about Kyle. She said she saw Kyle pacing back and forth by the side of his car and it was late at night. He looked behind him because something startled him, he saw this black figure with a hood, and he started running. He was terrified of the black hooded figure chasing him. She said his car was parked outside of a hotel. In her dream, he started running toward the highway and she saw him running across the highway, dodging cars. She saw the headlights of the truck coming toward him, but he didn't. Before the truck hit Kyle, she saw time stop and the truck stopped. She saw Kyle's spirit snatched out of his body and go up toward heaven, then the truck hit his body.

I believed God gave her the dream to let us know he felt no pain.

Although I am a seer, I wasn't supposed to see this. It was meant for my baby girl to see it.

The clairvoyant gift was passed down to the children. This may seem odd, but even Kyle had the gift as well, but I believed his gift became distorted when he moved out at 18. He never got a chance to mature the gift.

In other words, he saw too deep and when you see too deeply into the spiritual realm, it can be scary. I believed Kyle knew that his time was coming to an end, based on the things he said. When Kyle was running on that highway, I don't even think he realized the danger he was in. He was in such a paranoid state of mind, that he was just trying to get away.

They wrote in the newspaper article that he committed suicide. Kyle would never do that because he knew the Word of God. When he dropped Tasha off after lunch on Monday, he had gone job hunting. When Tasha finally got the car back, she saw he was at the library that day, looking for jobs.

My husband told me when Kyle was cutting his hair, about six weeks before he passed, he knew something was bothering him. He kept asking him what was wrong. Kyle said,

"Dad, if I told you and mom, it would scare you."

Bertram was persistent and kept telling Kyle he could tell him, so Kyle opened up. He said,

"I saw God. I saw my spirit going up out of my body into a bright light."

My husband said Tasha's cousin came down and interrupted the conversation and Kyle never got to finish. I think it was just Kyle's time and there was nothing anybody could do to stop it.

Later, Kashara was looking on the computer at the news and they had a picture of Kyle's red Corsica parked outside the Marriott, she called us down to see it. The Marriott was right off exit 23 off Interstate 91 South.

I was familiar with the area because Kayla was just about to start modeling school, right off exit 23, The John Casablanca Modeling Career Center. I would have to drive to that exit for the next 14 weeks, taking Kayla to modeling school.

We all got ready to go to church that night. Kashara, Kayla, Keenan, Natasha and me. Bertram stayed home. I picked Kevin up from Windsor Lock in East Windsor, Connecticut which was about fifteen minutes away from Enfield. I knew my Kevin was fragile because he was dealing with his own set of challenges. He was 20 years old at the time, and in a live-in care facility with other young adults dealing with mental health issues. Kevin had an emotional break when he was sixteen. In the past, he struggled with major depression and other mental health matters. Kevin had bottomed out so bad emotionally that he had to relearn how to eat, brush his teeth, dress himself, and the like. I needed us all to be together and ride together. I tried to talk about something other than the obvious elephant in the car, only because Kevin didn't know yet. When I finally broke the news, he listened intently and quietly.

I don't know if it were by habit or autopilot that we went to church that fateful Tuesday night, but there we were in the parking lot of the church. When we got there, I proceeded in and went to my seat in my usual place in the pulpit. I am one of the elders in the church. Tasha went in with probably just enough strength to make it to a seat in the back. I believed Tasha's mother; Vanessa told the Pastor what was going on and he pulled Tasha in the office to get an update and an understanding.

The church was in the devotional part of the service when the reality of everything came crashing down on Kayla. She bellowed out a wrenching cry and ran to the bathroom. I left out to be with her and comfort her. Pastor Leroy then came out and told me to take my family home. Tasha went home with her mom so she wouldn't be by herself. We headed back home. Suddenly, Keenan broke down on the way home. Keenan was 10 years old at this time. He saith that within a month of it happening, he dreamed the same dream Kayla dreamed. He told me he had a dream about Kyle's funeral service with the same picture Kyle had above his casket.

Unbeknownst to us at the time, Leete-Stevens Family Funeral would have Kyle's picture printed on the blanket as a gift to the family. Keenan saw that same picture in his dream, but he thought Kyle was a lot older when it happened. He also said he saw his brother's face in the television screen twice before his death. We all stayed around each other for the next week until the funeral services culminated.

Tasha and Noah were over every day. We supported each other with hugs and tears, and we talked a lot.

It was necessary for the siblings to be together for that emotional love and support. Kevin didn't need to deal with his brother's death without his own family. I spoke to his social worker, Cherie about our fragile situation. She gave her sympathy and said it would be fine for Kevin to come home for the week, so I picked him up daily. She also said they would make sure they provided supportive services for him.

Noah was like a son to Kyle, so the news of his demise hit him really hard. Noah came over to be with Keenan during the gathering of the family. They were like brothers so playing together was a regular occurrence with those two.

Once when I was driving him to the house, the little tyke was in the back seat talking to Keenan, just laughing. Noah is very smart, and he is very talkative at times. He repeated, "Uncle Kyle took me on a ride." He giggled on every memory of his uncle. I realized that our son left an indelible impression on Noah. Tasha says he constantly talks about Kyle. When the little one was once at the house, he sat on the couch and spoke about Kyle. He said he felt that his uncle is still with him, and pointed to his heart. I said to him, "He is with me in my heart too." That touched my heart deeply.

I know that he will never forget Kyle. The good values and happy memories Kyle left him will always be with him as he grows up and will overpower the negative ones of this devastating event. Noah really loved Kyle.

For the next three nights I couldn't sleep, but God ministered to me those nights. I visioned Kyle in his celestial (heavenly) form on that first night. God showed me, him in the third heavens all a glowing.

He said,

"Mom I am okay, I am free, and I am not in emotional pain anymore."

He was running and leaping for joy. He was so happy. I would have to say that even if Kyle could come back, he would not want to. Heaven is a beautiful and glorious place. No more pain or sorrow and God is going to wipe all our tears away.

Rev. 7:17 *"For the Lamb which is in the midst of the throne shall feed them and shall lead them unto living fountains of waters: and God shall wipe away all tears from their eyes."*

God brought back to my remembrance, how He prepared me for this day. He brought my mind back to the last six weeks of Kyle's life; on how he called me and said that his time was short, and he needed to get his life right with God. He said the sinner's prayer, then went to the altar and recommitted his life to Christ. He got everything right with his wife, and all the crying he did those last few weeks allowed him to get rid of all that anger and frustration that had accumulated in his heart.

That Friday night when he came to the house because he thought someone was out to kill him, was the first time I knew how much Satan was tormenting him in his mind. Kyle was able to stay one last week with the family; this was all in God's divine plan. I had a vivid memory of all these things. God was preparing me for this time. The Lord will never let things sneak up on his servants if they are prayerful.

Everything became so cleared to me, and I understood why God allowed everything to unfold as it did.

He took me back to the time of Kyle's birth, when the umbilical cord was wrapped around his neck seven times, and how his life could have been taken then. I thought about how Hannah, in the Bible, had given Samuel back to the Lord when he was born.

Our children don't belong to us, they belong to God. He just lends them to us for a period of time. Not all of us are guaranteed long lives. I was grateful to God for lending Kyle to us for 23 years and how he had become a great part of all our lives. I have so many good precious memories of my son that no one can ever take them away. Kyle made my life so rich. I am so grateful to God for the time he had allowed Kyle to spend with us, and all the joy he brought us.

Kyle had such a big, kind, and compassionate heart and he loved people. Kyle loved God and always wanted to do the right thing. When he was alive, he touched so many people's lives.

He had a huge homegoing service. I never had anyone come up to me and say anything bad about Kyle, they always told me what a nice, kind young man he was. He was always obedient to us, and he never gave us any problems growing up. May the life I live, speak for me. God has a purpose and a plan for all our lives.

Ecclesiastics 3:1-2 *"To everything there is a season and a time to every purpose under the heaven. A time to be born, and a time to die."*

No one can change our destiny. It's all in God's

hands. So, we should live life to the best of our ability, according to God's Word and will.

Some things just baffle my mind when I think about how things happened. On the night Kyle died, I was driving on Interstate 91, coming back from taking my oldest sister, Gloria home. She was the children's second mom because she helped take care of them while I worked at Mercy Hospital. I took her home when I got out of work which made me get home even later.

I was on the same highway driving at the exact time the truck struck my son. I was in Enfield, and he was in Rocky Hill.

Also, when I got off work that morning, at 1 a.m., Evangelist Sherry Rex left me a message on my cell phone to call her back, no matter what time I got off work because she needed to talk to me.

When I called her back, she picked right up. She said,

"I am glad you called me back because I had this dream I needed to tell you about. When God gives me dreams, it means something. I had a dream that I was at the bank trying to draw money out and they wouldn't let me. I knew I had money in there. You were with me in the dream, so we started walking down the street. We came to this big vacant building, and we went in. When we went in the building, there were three boys lying on the floor, dead. We began to pray, and the three boys rose up. The first boy was tall and thin, the second medium built, and the third boy was shorter and younger. All three boys were fully dressed, but none of them had on shoes. We all walked down the street together. The tall thin boy kept talking about all the spiritual warfare he was going through. You were telling him it was going to be all right. I want you to think about the interpretation of that dream. I am going to write it down and pray for interpretation also." We talked a little longer and hung up.

I thought about her dream and supernaturally, I knew immediately, who the three boys were. They were my sons, Kyle, Kevin and Keenan. The boy talking about the spiritual warfare was Kyle. We later discussed the dream, and she said God had given her the dream's interpretation. Yes, she said the three boys were my sons and that God was going to raise up a ministry out of all three of them. The reason they had no shoes on was because they all had a different path to walk. She said even though Kyle died, a ministry will still come out of his life. Amazing! Look at God!

All the extended family were incredibly supportive during this time. We were getting calls from family and friends from all over the country.

Michael, my brother and his wife, Sandra called and gave their condolences. They live in South Carolina, and are Kyle's God parents. They wouldn't make it to the service because they had been up a couple of times in the same year for our other relatives who had passed away.

The house was filled with the church members, bringing food, drinks, and being supportive. Leroy, my brother The Pastor was extremely supportive. I could tell he felt like maybe he didn't do enough as a pastor. Immediately, I let him know, it was Kyle's time and there was nothing anybody could have done to stop it.

Leete-Stevens Family Funeral Home did Kyle's service. Sean Stevens was the funeral director who collaborated with us and did a beautiful job. We are eternally grateful to he and his family for all their compassion and hard work to make things go smoothly. Kyle's homegoing was huge. A lot of his classmates from high school came.

Everybody from his wedding party came and some of my co-workers from the hospital came. A lot of the doctors, nurses, management, and other co-workers were wonderfully supportive. Many family members, church members, and numerous people I can't even name, showed us a lot of love and support.

Natasha picked the following poem for the service.

"I AM FREE"
Don't grieve for me for now I'm free,
I'm following the path God laid for me
I took his hand when I heard him call,
I turned my back and left it all
I could not stay another day,
To laugh, to love, to work or play
Tasks left undone must stay that way,
I've found that peace at the close of day
If my parting has left a void,
Then fill it with remembered joy
A friendship shared, a laugh, a kiss,
Ah yes, these things I too will miss
Be not burdened with times of sorrow,
I wish for you the sunshine of tomorrow
My life's been full, I've savored much,
Good friends, good times, my loved one's touch
If my time seemed all too brief,
Don't lengthen it now with undue grief
Lift up your heart, rejoice with me,

God wanted me now, He set me free.
~ *By Anne Lindgren Davison*

The Pallbearers were Amahd Elliot (cousin), Clifton Stovall (cousin), Cory Stovall (cousin), George Stovall (uncle), Michael Meadows (brother of the church) and Veral Elliot (uncle). Pastor Stovall officiated the service at Holy Ghost Temple Church, 30 Massasoit Ave, West Springfield, MA 01089.

Donations in Kyle's memory can still be made to the ministry H.G. T. Prayer and Deliverance Radio Ministry P.O. Box 362- Enfield, Ct 06083.

Website:www.vivianrobinson.org

Kyle had a closed casket and was laid to rest at Hazardville Cemetery on December 22, 2009.

CHAPTER 9

The Visitation

After Kyle passed, he appeared to all his siblings in his celestial form to provide comfort. Keenan was in the bathroom combing his hair when he said he saw Kyle's face in the mirror, glowing. He was smiling and looked happy. He said to Keenan, "Tell the family I am okay, and listen to mom and dad." He appeared to Kayla in a dream. She dreamed she was sitting on the front pew in the church and Kyle came and sat by her. He was smiling and glowing. He put his arm around her and told her he was okay. She asked him why he had to leave, and he said it was his time. Kashara said she saw him while she was dancing in church one Sunday morning. She said he was dressed in a white suit, glowing all over and smiling. He had two wings behind him. She said he looked so happy and handsome. He told her not to worry because he was okay.

When Kyle first died, some people thought it was Kevin. He even felt guilty, at one time, and wanted to know why God didn't take him instead of Kyle. He was even angry at God, so, I really had to minister to him a lot. I told him that God was too wise to make a mistake. It was Kyle's time. God had work for Kevin to do. I told him once he was able to find peace with Kyle's death, he would be able to feel his brother's presence. So, it took Kevin about three months to come to terms with his brother's death. After three months, Kevin dreamed about Kyle. He said he saw Kyle dressed in all white, glowing and smiling. He looked happy. He told Kevin not to worry about him because he was okay. Kyle told him it was time for him to step up to the plate. He was the oldest boy now, so he needed to help take care of the family, pull himself together and go back to church.

My husband took our son's death the hardest. I think it had been two weeks since he had seen Kyle before he passed. I am sure that haunted him. Every time he heard Kyle's name mentioned, he would get teary-eyed and upset. So, I tried not to mention Kyle's name around him. We all grieve differently. About nine months after Kyle passed, Bertram was at the gym working out. He and Kyle used to work out at the gym together. They use to spot each other when lifting weights. This day, Bertram was lifting weights. When he took a break and sat up, he said he felt Kyle brush by him.

 Kyle appeared to Tasha, his wife, about five months after he passed. She was at church, standing while the word was being preached. Kyle appeared to her, and he was glowing, smiling, and looked very happy. He told her he was okay and that she was going to be okay. He told her, "Everything is going to be alright." She said she often feels his presence around the house, especially when she is feeling down, he'll let her know it is going to be okay.

The first three days, when I was lying in bed and couldn't sleep, I asked the Lord why his death was made so public. It was all on the television news and in the newspaper. God let me know, what the devil meant for bad, God would turn it around for the good; for such a time as this, for the writing of this book.

Our testimony is our life story. This book is Kyle's journey of his life story. What a testimony!

May it touch, transform, and comfort millions of people's lives as they read it.

I went back to work two weeks after Kyle's death.

I had to minister to a lot of people because they did not understand why he was taken so young. Especially the unbelievers because they viewed it as such a tragic death. They did not understand why I was not totally distraught, but was still laughing and smiling. A lot of people thought he committed suicide because of the newspapers. Some people just looked at me and started crying, some just hugged me, and some didn't say anything at all because they didn't know what to say. All I know is I was at peace because I love and trust God. I know Kyle is up in heaven smiling and rejoicing and I can feel his presence from time to time. When I start missing him, I hear him saying,

"Mom, I'm okay."

Kyle is in a different realm, now. He is watching over his wife, Natasha; being the protector, no more naturally, but as an immortal (celestial) being. He's also watching over his family.

Philippians 1:21, *"For to me, to live is Christ and to die is gain." We gain eternal life when we die in Christ.*

After working for 25 years at the hospital, as a registered nurse, I decided to work for six months longer, then retire. I made my exodus June 16,

2010.

Kyle's death made me realize how short life really is. Only what we do for Christ will last. It was time for me to do what God had instructed me to do. It was time for me to go full throttle. So I went full-time in ministry because there are so many souls that still need to hear the message of salvation. Jesus commissioned me to go out into the hedges and highways and compel them to come to Christ, (**St Luke 14:23**)

Theoretically, Kyle would want his mother to continue doing ministry. When someone leaves us, life goes on. So, while that individual is alive, that is your time to value them and do all you can for them. Then when they are gone, you will have no regrets. I had given compassion to a Godly work of nursing for 39 years of my life, and now it is time to give God my life in a different capacity.

I don't know where my journey with Christ will take me, what I do know is, I must keep walking the path He has chosen for me and continue to trust Him. When my time is up, I will join Kyle in Heaven and rejoice with him along with the other saints gone on before me.

EPILOGUE

If there were one thing, one suggestion I would render, one thought I would share, it would be this: DON'T SUFFER IN SILENCE.

If you suspect a loved one or even yourself having signs and symptoms of a deeper issue, please sit and talk to somebody.

If you have a loved one, or if you have challenges with seeing images, hearing voices, anger or rage issues, depression, mood swings, grief, substance abuse, panic attacks, paranoia, these are overt signs of a deeper issue.

Mental health is just as important in a person's life as physical health. God made the body, but the body has its issues in the blood, muscles, ligaments, cells, tissues, bones, organs, vascular, respiratory, nerves, and skin because of environment, abuse, ignorance, heredity, and other causes.

God made our bodies to heal itself, but sometimes we may have to get other sources to assist us to get our physical health back on track. So is the same thing with the emotional and mental health.

You can be physically healthy, but mentally ill. You can be the opposite of the former example, or you can be both mentally and physically ill.

God wishes that we be in health and prosper in our soul.

We are three partite beings and are made up of these three components: spirit, soul, and body. The real you, the spirit, is the thing that is all like God. We are spirit. We have a soul which houses the mind, will, emotion, intellect, and imagination, and we live in a body (earth suit).

If you ignore the natural side of healing for any part of the body, you could perish. And the same holds true for the spiritual side. If it's all God and no intervention or attention paid to any part of the body, you could perish.

Understand the professionals are just God's assistants. They can help you see what you can't see. They can help you to understand triggers in the actions or reaction of a person's psyche.

Don't be afraid to talk about what is feared the most. Don't live in silent pain or torment. Get help. Get your loved one help.

Here is the toll free number for help. They can

direct you in your particular city and state.

If you or someone you know is in crisis, please **call 911 or 211!**

go to the nearest emergency room

call **1-800-273-TALK (8255)** to reach a 24-hour crisis center

text MHA to 741741 at the Crisis Text Line.

If you need to talk but not in a crisis, contact warmline.org

We pray peace, calmness, wholeness, wellness, and the unction to know when you are not ok, to get to a trained professional, a trusted member of your family, or a confidant, or a church that is both secular on matters of counseling and spirituality with prayers and follow through plans to help a person reach his best potential of healing.

ABOUT THE AUTHOR

Vivian S. Robinson was born in Montgomery, Alabama 1963. She graduated from Holyoke High School, attended New England Baptist School of nursing in Boston, MA from 1982-1985, and graduated as a Registered Nurse. She has been in the nursing profession for more than 20 years. Prophetess Vivian Robinson married her childhood sweet heart in 1988 and has been married for more than 36 years. They have five lovely children, three boys and two girls, of which Kyle preceded them in death.

Prophetess Robinson have strong roots in the church and the religious community. She has served in ministry for 35 years working her way up the ranks. She started as an usher, then a secretary, choir director, Sunday school teacher, President of the Youth Department for six years and President of the Women's Department for 5 years.

Finally, God called her into pulpit ministry first as an Evangelist at age 25 and second into the prophetic ministry at age 27. She has done outdoor ministry for many years such as volunteering and serving meals at the shelter, visiting and praying for patients in nursing homes and the hospitals. She has done outdoor and indoor revivals. Prophetess Robinson has done public T.V. ministry for 16 years with the late Co-Pastor Eugenia Stovall, editing and producing their own shows. She has hosted her own radio show called Holy Grace Temple Prayer & Deliverance Outreach Ministry for 15 years.

She was with WACE radio ministry in Chicopee, MA which covers most of New England about 15 years. Currently she is with podcast under Prophetess Vivian Robinson, and you can google for her teachings. Go to her website www.vivianrobinson.org and she is on multiple social media platforms:

Prophetess Vivian Robinson finished with WHAP which is THE POINT RADIO AM/FM in Hopewell, VA in 2023.

In the past, she has been with three other radio ministries such as WELP, out of Greenville, SC, WNVY, which is out of Pensacola, FL and lastly, WDZY, AM/FM, which is located in Richmond, VA. Her future goals are to open up more ministries.

Along with radio ministries, she has internet ministries with Facebook and YouTube, website: www.vivianrobinson.org

In the year 2018, she began missionary work with Haiti

and Africa, she has been doing missionary work with
Kenya for 6 years and is currently devising a plan to erect a
medical clinic in the location of Nyamira.

Reverend Vivian Robinson is an ordained elder under the
auspices of Bishop W.E. Summerlin Sr. Prior to her
appointment to Free and Accepted Holiness Church of
God in Montgomery Alabama, she followed the leadership
of Bishop Leroy Stovall at Holy Ghost Temple Church for
about 40 years. Elder Vivian Robinson received all of her
mentoring from Bishop Leroy and late Co-Pastor Eugenia
Stovall. She states her Bishop as an excellent teacher and a
great inspiration to her ministry.

She enjoys family, reading and ministering.

www.ingramcontent.com/pod-product-compliance
Lightning Source LLC
Chambersburg PA
CBHW070533160726
48003CB00004B/1774